Preface

Azure AI Fundamentals AI 900 Certification Guide is designed to provide a comprehensive introduction to the foundational principles of Artificial Intelligence (AI) and its applications within the Microsoft Azure ecosystem. As AI continues to drive technological advancements across industries, gaining a fundamental understanding of its principles and practical implementations has become essential for professionals, decision-makers, students, and technology enthusiasts alike. This certification serves as an entry point for individuals seeking to explore AI concepts, including machine learning, computer vision, natural language processing, and conversational AI, while also gaining hands-on experience with Azure AI services such as Azure Cognitive Services, Azure Machine Learning, and Azure Bot Services. Through a structured and accessible approach, this guide demystifies complex AI concepts, ensuring that learners from diverse backgrounds can grasp the essential elements of AI and its integration within Azure.

Beyond serving as a preparatory resource for the AI-900 certification exam, this book is crafted to provide practical insights into how AI solutions can be leveraged effectively in real-world scenarios. Each chapter is meticulously structured to build upon key concepts, offering both theoretical understanding and applied knowledge through practical exercises. Whether you are an IT professional aiming to integrate AI into cloud solutions, a business leader seeking to understand AI's strategic implications, or a student eager to explore AI fundamentals, Microsoft Azure AI Fundamentals (AI-900) Certification Guide serves as an indispensable resource. It is our hope that this book not only prepares you for the certification but also fosters a deeper appreciation for AI's transformative potential, equipping you with the knowledge and confidence to navigate the evolving landscape of artificial intelligence.

Table of Contents

Chapter 1: Introduction of Azure AI Fundamentals AI- 900

Microsoft Corporation: Microsoft is a multinational technology company that is a major player in the software, hardware, and technology solutions industry. It was founded in 1975 by Bill Gates and Paul Allen and has since become a global leader in the development of software, operating systems, cloud computing, and various other technological innovations. Microsoft's products include the Windows operating system, Microsoft Office suite, Azure cloud platform, and a wide range of software applications and services.

Microsoft Certification: Microsoft offers a comprehensive certification program that validates the skills and expertise of IT professionals and developers across various Microsoft products and technologies. Microsoft certifications cover a wide range of roles, including system administration, development, data analysis, cloud computing, security, and more. These certifications are designed to provide a structured path for individuals to acquire and demonstrate proficiency in Microsoft technologies.

Links of all certifications: -

https://learn.microsoft.com/en-us/credentials/browse/?credential_types=certification

Value of Microsoft Certification:

1. Industry Recognition: Microsoft certifications are widely recognized in the IT industry, and achieving certification demonstrates your competence and expertise in using Microsoft technologies.
2. Skills Validation: Microsoft certification exams are rigorous and cover practical aspects of using Microsoft products and services. Successfully passing these exams validates your skills and knowledge in specific areas.
3. Career Advancement: Microsoft certifications are valuable for career advancement. They can enhance your employability, open new job opportunities, and potentially lead to promotions within your current organization.
4. Competitive Edge: In a competitive job market, having Microsoft certifications can give you a competitive edge. Employers often prefer candidates with validated skills and certifications, especially when considering applicants for roles involving Microsoft technologies.

5. Structured Learning Path: Microsoft certifications are organized into role-based and product-specific learning paths. These paths provide a structured approach to gaining expertise, starting from fundamental skills to more advanced topics.

6. Stay Current with Technology: Microsoft frequently updates its certifications to align with the latest advancements in technology. By pursuing and maintaining Microsoft certifications, professionals can stay current with industry trends and evolving technologies.

7. Community and Resources: Certification programs often come with access to a community of certified professionals and additional resources, including forums, training materials, and events, fostering continuous learning and networking opportunities.

Certification Levels: Microsoft certifications are categorized into different levels, including:

• Fundamental: Entry-level certifications suitable for beginners or those with basic knowledge.

• Associate: Intermediate certifications requiring a deeper understanding of the technology.

• Expert: Advanced certifications for professionals with extensive experience and expertise.

Specialty: Certifications that focus on specific roles or domains within a technology area.

What is AI-900?

https://learn.microsoft.com/en-us/credentials/certifications/exams/ai-900/

The AI-900 certification is designed for those who are new to AI and want to explore its fundamental concepts and applications. Microsoft Azure, one of the leading cloud platforms, offers a comprehensive suite of AI services, and the AI-900 certification introduces participants to the basics of AI, machine learning, and how these technologies are integrated into Azure.

Why Use Microsoft Azure AI?

Microsoft Azure AI provides a robust and scalable platform for the development and deployment of AI solutions. Whether you are a developer, IT professional, or business decision-maker, understanding Azure AI can empower you to leverage AI technologies to solve real-world problems, drive innovation, and enhance business operations.

Benefits of AI-900 Certification:

1. Foundational Knowledge: The certification offers a foundational understanding of AI concepts, making it accessible to beginners and professionals from various backgrounds.

2. Azure AI Services: Gain insights into the diverse range of AI services offered by Azure, including cognitive services, machine learning, and natural language processing.

3. Career Opportunities: The certification can open doors to various roles within the AI domain, including AI engineer, data scientist, and business intelligence professional.

4. Industry Recognition: Being a Microsoft certification, AI-900 is globally recognized, providing validation of your knowledge and skills in the AI domain.

How to Use Microsoft Azure AI:

1. Learning Path: Begin by following a structured learning path that covers the AI-900 exam objectives. Microsoft provides official learning materials, including documentation, videos, and hands-on labs.

2. Hands-On Experience: Azure AI is best learned through practical experience. Engage with the Azure portal to experiment with AI services, build and deploy models, and gain hands-on proficiency.

3. Practice Exams: Utilize practice exams to assess your knowledge and readiness for the certification. Microsoft offers official practice tests to help you prepare for the AI-900 exam.

4. Community and Resources: Join online forums, discussion groups, and the Microsoft Learn community to connect with peers and access additional resources for continuous learning.

What is the price of this certification:

Link is given below and further information are also here:

https://learn.microsoft.com/en-us/credentials/certifications/azure-ai-fundamentals/

and how much Score to achieved in this certification exam:

Passing score: 700/1000.

How to access your score report: - https://learn.microsoft.com/en-us/credentials/certifications/exam-scoring-reports#scores-needed-to-pass-exams

Conclusion:

The Microsoft Azure AI Fundamentals (AI-900) certification provides a gateway for individuals to explore the world of AI on one of the leading cloud platforms. Whether you are a developer, IT professional, or business leader, the foundational knowledge gained through this certification can set the stage for further specialization and career advancement in the rapidly evolving field of artificial intelligence. Embrace the opportunities that AI-900 offers to enhance your understanding of AI concepts and leverage the capabilities of Microsoft Azure for intelligent and innovative solutions.

Chapter 2: Features of Book:

- Explore foundational concepts of Azure AI.
- Understand the cloud-based nature of Azure AI solutions.
- Provide an overview of various AI services in Azure.
- Explore the wide range of Azure Cognitive Services.
- Understand their collective role in AI application development.
- Dive into Computer Vision and Face API.
- Learn practical applications and use cases for vision services.
- Explore Text Analytics, Translator, and Speech Services.
- Understand how language services enhance AI applications.
- Introduce Azure Cognitive Search and QnA Maker.
- Discuss how decision services contribute to intelligent solutions.
- Provide hands-on coding examples for practical learning.
- Explore techniques for image analysis and recognition.
- Discuss best practices for image-related solutions.
- Discuss language translation services and applications.
- Highlight the role of Azure Translator in multilingual applications.
- Guide on creating Q&A services for AI applications.
- Discuss best practices in crafting effective Q&A models.
- Introduce the fundamentals of Azure Machine Learning.
- Explore the role of Azure ML in building AI solutions.
- Guide on building and training machine learning models.
- Cover considerations for model selection and optimization.
- Explain the deployment process using Azure ML.
- Discuss best practices for deploying models as RESTful APIs.
- Summarize best practices derived from practical experiences.
- Discuss lessons learned from both successful and challenging AI implementations.
- Recommend study strategies and resources for exam preparation.
- Provide a roadmap for focused and efficient study sessions.
- Include practice exam questions to help readers assess their readiness.

- Present realistic scenarios to reinforce key concepts.

Chapter 3: Questions of Microsoft Azure AI Fundamentals Exam AI-900 Part 1

Question 1. A company employs a team of customer service agents to provide telephone and email support to customers.

The company develops a webchat bot to provide automated answers to common customer queries.

Which business benefit should the company expect as a result of creating the webchat bot solution?

A. increased sales

B. a reduced workload for the customer service agents

C. improved product reliability

Answer: B

Question 2. For a machine learning progress, how should you split data for training and evaluation?

A. Use features for training and labels for evaluation.

B. Randomly split the data into rows for training and rows for evaluation.

C. Use labels for training and features for evaluation.

D. Randomly split the data into columns for training and columns for evaluation.

Answer: B

Question 3. You build a machine learning model by using the automated machine learning user interface (UI).

You need to ensure that the model meets the Microsoft transparency principle for responsible AI.

What should you do?

A. Set Validation type to Auto.

B. Enable Explain best model.

C. Set Primary metric to accuracy.

D. Set Max concurrent iterations to 0.

Answer: B

Question 4. HOTSPOT –

For each of the following statements, select Yes if the statement is true. Otherwise, select No.

NOTE: Each correct selection is worth one point.

Hot Area:

Statements	Yes	No
A. Forecasting housing prices based on historical data is an example of anomaly detection.		
B. Identifying suspicious sign-ins by looking for deviations from usual patterns is an example of anomaly detection.		
C. Predicting whether a patient will develop diabetes based on the patient's medical history is an example of anomaly detection.		

Answer: A: No, B: Yes, C: No

Question 5. To complete the sentence, select the appropriate option in the answer area.

Hot Area:

The handle of unusual or missing values provided to an AI System is a consideration for the Microsoft

A. Inclusiveness
B. Privacy & Security
C. Reliability & safety.
D. Transparency

Principle for responsible AI.

Answer: C

Question 6. You are designing an AI system that empowers everyone, including people who have hearing, visual, and other impairments.

This is an example of which Microsoft guiding principle for responsible AI?

A. fairness

B. inclusiveness

C. reliability and safety

D. accountability

Answer. B

Question 7. You are building an AI system.

Which task should you include to ensure that the service meets the Microsoft transparency principle for responsible AI?

A. Ensure that all visuals have an associated text that can be read by a screen reader.

B. Enable autoscaling to ensure that a service-scales based on demand.

C. Provide documentation to help developers debug code.

D. Ensure that a training dataset is representative of the population.

Answer: C

Question 8. What are three Microsoft guiding principles for responsible AI? Each correct answer presents a complete solution.

NOTE: Each correct selection is worth one point.

A. knowledgeability

B. decisiveness

C. inclusiveness

D. fairness

E. opinionatedness

F. reliability and safety

Answer: C, D, F

Question 9. You run a charity event that involves posting photos of people wearing sunglasses on Twitter.

You need to ensure that you only retweet photos that meet the following requirements:

- Include one or more faces.
- Contain at least one person wearing sunglasses.

What should you use to analyze the images?

A. The Verify operation in the Face service

B. The Detect operation in the Face service

C. The Describe Image operation in the Computer Vision service

D. The Analyze Image operation in the Computer Vision service

Answer: B

Question 10. When you design an AI system to assess whether loans should be approved, the factors used to make the decision should be explainable.

This is an example of which Microsoft guiding principle for responsible AI?

A. transparency

B. inclusiveness

C. fairness

D. privacy and security

Answer: A

Question 11. You are building an AI-based app.

You need to ensure that the app uses the principles for responsible AI.

Which two principles should you follow? Each correct answer presents part of the solution.

NOTE: Each correct selection is worth one point.

A. Implement an Agile software development methodology

B. Implement a process of AI model validation as part of the software review process

C. Establish a risk governance committee that includes members of the legal team, members of the risk management team, and a privacy officer

D. Prevent the disclosure of the use of AI-based algorithms for automated decision making.

Answer: B, C

Question 12. To complete the sentence, select the appropriate option in the answer area.

Hot Area:

A. Dependent variables
B. Features
C. Identifiers
D. Labels

Data values that influence the prediction of a model are called

Answer: B

Question 13. Which type of machine learning should you use to predict the number of gift cards that will be sold next month?

A. classification

B. regression

C. clustering

Answer: B

Question 14. You have a dataset that contains information about taxi journeys that occurred during a given period.

You need to train a model to predict the fare of a taxi journey.

What should you use as a feature?

A. the number of taxi journeys in the dataset

B. the trip distance of individual taxi journeys

C. the fare of individual taxi journeys

D. the trip ID of individual taxi journeys

Answer: B

Question 15. You need to predict the sea level in meters for the next 10 years.

Which type of machine learning should you use?

A. classification

B. regression

C. clustering

Answer: B

Question 16: For each of the following statements, select Yes if the statement is true. Otherwise, select No.

NOTE: Each correct selection is worth one point.

Hot Area:

Statements	Yes	No
A. Automated machine learning is the process of automating the time- consuming, iterative tasks of machine learning model development.		
B. Automated machine learning can automatically infer the training data from the use case provided.		
C. Automated machine learning works by running multiple training iterations that are scored and ranked by the metrics you specify-		
D. Automated machine learning enables you to specify a dataset and will automatically understand which label to predict		

Answer:

Statements	Yes / No
A. Automated machine learning is the process of automating the time-consuming, iterative tasks of machine learning model development.	Yes
B. Automated machine learning can automatically infer the training data from the use case provided.	No
C. Automated machine learning works by running multiple training iterations that are scored and ranked by the metrics you specify-	Yes
D. Automated machine learning enables you to specify a dataset and will automatically understand which label to predict	No

Question 17. To complete the sentence, select the appropriate option in the answer area.

Hot Area:

A banking system that predicts whether a loan will be repaid is an example of the

A. Classification
B. Regression
C. Clustering

type of machine learning.

Answer: A

Question 18. Which service should you use to extract text, key/value pairs, and table data automatically from scanned documents?

A. Form Recognizer

B. Text Analytics

C. Language Understanding

D. Custom Vision

Answer: A

Question 19. You are designing an AI system that empowers everyone, including people who have hearing, visual, and other impairments.

This is an example of which Microsoft guiding principle for responsible AI?

A. fairness

B. inclusiveness

C. reliability and safety

D. accountability

Answer: B

Question 20. You are building an AI system.

Which task should you include to ensure that the service meets the Microsoft transparency principle for responsible AI?

A. Ensure that all visuals have an associated text that can be read by a screen reader.

B. Enable autoscaling to ensure that a service-scales based on demand.

C. Provide documentation to help developers debug code.

D. Ensure that a training dataset is representative of the population.

Answer: C

Question 21. A company employs a team of customer service agents to provide telephone and email support to customers. The company develops a webchat bot to provide automated answers to common customer queries.

Which business benefit should the company expect as a result of creating the webchat bot solution?

A. increased sales

B. a reduced workload for the customer service agents

C. improved product reliability

Answer: B

Question 22. You build a machine learning model by using the automated machine learning user interface (UI). You need to ensure that the model meets the Microsoft transparency principle for responsible AI. What should you do?

A. Set Validation type to Auto.

B. Enable Explain best model.

C. Set Primary metric to accuracy.

D. Set Max concurrent iterations to 0.

Answer: B

Question 23. For each of the following statements, select Yes if the statement is true. Otherwise, select No.

NOTE: Each correct selection is worth one point.

Statements	Yes	No
A. Forecasting housing prices based on historical data is an example of anomaly detection.		
B. Identifying suspicious sign-ins by looking for deviations from usual patterns is an example of anomaly detection.		
C. Predicting whether a patient will develop diabetes based on the patient's medical history is an example of anomaly detection.		

A. Mastered

B. Not Mastered

Answer: A

Box 1: No Box 2: Yes Box 3: Yes

Question 24. What are three Microsoft guiding principles for responsible AI? Each correct answer presents a complete solution.

NOTE: Each correct selection is worth one point.

A. knowledgeability

B. decisiveness

C. inclusiveness

D. fairness

E. opinionatedness

F. reliability and safety

Answer: CDF

Question 25. Which two components can you drag onto a canvas in Azure Machine Learning designer? Each correct answer presents a complete solution.

NOTE: Each correct selection is worth one point.

A. dataset

B. compute

C. pipeline

D. module

Answer: AD

Question 26. You need to predict the income range of a given customer by using the following dataset.

Which two fields should you use as features? Each correct answer presents a complete solution.

NOTE: Each correct selection is worth one point.

First Name	Last Name	Age	Educational Level	Income Range
Orlando	Gee	45	University	25,000-50,000
Keith	Harris	36	High school	25,000-50,000
Donna	Carreras	52	University	50,000-75,000
Janet	Gates	21	University	75,000-100,000
Lucy	Harrington	68	High school	50,000-75,000

A. Education Level

B. Last Name

C. Age

D. Income Range

E. First Name

Answer: AC

Question 27. You are designing an AI system that empowers everyone, including people who have hearing, visual, and other impairments.

This is an example of which Microsoft guiding principle for responsible AI?

A. fairness

B. inclusiveness

C. reliability and safety

D. accountability

Answer: B

Question 28. You are building an AI system.

Which task should you include to ensure that the service meets the Microsoft transparency principle for responsible AI?

A. Ensure that all visuals have an associated text that can be read by a screen reader.

B. Enable autoscaling to ensure that a service scales based on demand.

C. Provide documentation to help developers debug code.

D. Ensure that a training dataset is representative of the population.

Answer: C

Question 30. A company employs a team of customer service agents to provide telephone and email support to customers. The company develops a webchat bot to provide automated answers to common customer queries.

Which business benefit should the company expect as a result of creating the webchat bot solution?

A. increased sales

B. a reduced workload for the customer service agents

C. improved product reliability

Answer: B

Question 31. To complete the sentence, select the appropriate option in the answer area.

A. Feature Engineering
B. Feature selection
C. Model evaluation
D. Model Training

is used to generate additional features.

A. Mastered

B. Not Mastered

Answer: A

Question 32. You build a machine learning model by using the automated machine learning user interface (UI). You need to ensure that the model meets the Microsoft transparency principle for responsible AI. What should you do?

A. Set Validation type to Auto.

B. Enable Explain best model.

C. Set Primary metric to accuracy.

D. Set Max concurrent iterations to 0.

Answer: B

Question 33. What are three Microsoft guiding principles for responsible AI? Each correct answer presents a complete solution.

NOTE: Each correct selection is worth one point.

A. knowledgeability

B. decisiveness

C. inclusiveness

D. fairness

E. opinionatedness

F. reliability and safety

Answer: CDF

Question 34. Which two components can you drag onto a canvas in Azure Machine Learning designer? Each correct answer presents a complete solution.

NOTE: Each correct selection is worth one point.

A. dataset

B. compute

C. pipeline

D. module

Answer: AD

Question 35. You build a machine learning model by using the automated machine learning user interface (UI). You need to ensure that the model meets the Microsoft transparency principle for responsible AI. What should you do?

A. Set Validation type to Auto.

B. Enable Explain best model.

C. Set Primary metric to accuracy.

D. Set Max concurrent iterations to 0.

Answer: B

Question 36. What are three Microsoft guiding principles for responsible AI? Each correct answer presents a complete solution.

NOTE: Each correct selection is worth one point.

A. knowledgeability

B. decisiveness

C. inclusiveness

D. fairness

E. opinionatedness

F. reliability and safety

Answer: CDF

Question 37. Which type of machine learning should you use to predict the number of gift cards that will be sold next month?

A. classification

B. regression

C. clustering

Answer: C

Question 38. For each of the following statements, select Yes if the statement is true. Otherwise, select No. NOTE: Each correct selection is worth one point.

Statements	Yes	No
A. Automated machine learning provides you with the ability to Include custom Python scripts in a training pipeline.		
B. Automated machine learning implements machine learning solutions without the need for programming experience.		
C. Automated machine learning provides you with the ability to visually connect datasets and modules on an interactive canvas.		

A. Mastered

B. Not Mastered

Answer: A

Question 39. You build a machine learning model by using the automated machine learning user interface (UI). You need to ensure that the model meets the Microsoft transparency principle for responsible AI. What should you do?

A. Set Validation type to Auto.

B. Enable Explain best model.

C. Set Primary metric to accuracy.

D. Set Max concurrent iterations to 0.

Answer: B

Question 40. What are three Microsoft guiding principles for responsible AI? Each correct answer presents a complete solution.

NOTE: Each correct selection is worth one point.

A. knowledgeability

B. decisiveness

C. inclusiveness

D. fairness

E. opinionatedness

F. reliability and safety

Answer: CDF

Question 41. Which type of machine learning should you use to predict the number of gift cards that will be sold next month?

A. classification

B. regression

C. clustering

Answer: C

Question 42. You run a charity event that involves posting photos of people wearing sunglasses on Twitter. You need to ensure that you only retweet photos that meet the following requirements: Include one or more faces.

Contain at least one person wearing sunglasses. What should you use to analyze the images?

A. the Verify operation in the Face service

B. the Detect operation in the Face service

C. the Describe Image operation in the Computer Vision service

D. the Analyze Image operation in the Computer Vision service

Answer: B

Question 43. You build a machine learning model by using the automated machine learning user interface (UI). You need to ensure that the model meets the Microsoft transparency principle for responsible AI. What should you do?

A. Set Validation type to Auto.

B. Enable Explain best model.

C. Set Primary metric to accuracy.

D. Set Max concurrent iterations to 0.

Answer: B

Question 44. Match the Microsoft guiding principles for responsible AI to the appropriate descriptions.

To answer, drag the appropriate principle from the column on the left to its description on the right. Each principle may be used once, more than once, or not at all.

NOTE: Each correct selection is worth one point.

A. Mastered

B. Not Mastered

Answer: A

Question 45. Which metric can you use to evaluate a classification model?

A. true positive rate

B. mean absolute error (MAE)

C. coefficient of determination (R2)

D. root mean squared error (RMSE)

Answer: A

Question 46. Which type of machine learning should you use to predict the number of gift cards that will be sold next month?

A. classification

B. regression

C. clustering

Answer: C

Question 47. You need to predict the income range of a given customer by using the following dataset.

Which two fields should you use as features? Each correct answer presents a complete solution.

NOTE: Each correct selection is worth one point.

A. Education Level

B. Last Name

C. Age

D. Income Range

E. First Name

Answer: AC

Question 48. You build a machine learning model by using the automated machine learning user interface (UI). You need to ensure that the model meets the Microsoft transparency principle for responsible AI. What should you do?

A. Set Validation type to Auto.

B. Enable Explain best model.

C. Set Primary metric to accuracy.

D. Set Max concurrent iterations to 0.

Answer: B

Question 49. Your company is exploring the use of voice recognition technologies in its smart home devices. The company wants to identify any barriers that might unintentionally leave out specific user groups.

This an example of which Microsoft guiding principle for responsible AI?

A. accountability

B. fairness

C. inclusiveness

D. privacy and security

Answer: C

Question 50. Which metric can you use to evaluate a classification model?

A. true positive rate

B. mean absolute error (MAE)

C. coefficient of determination (R2)

D. root mean squared error (RMSE)

Answer: A

Question 50. Which type of machine learning should you use to predict the number of gift cards that will be sold next month?

A. classification

B. regression

C. clustering

Answer: C

Question 51. You use Azure Machine Learning designer to publish an inference pipeline.

Which two parameters should you use to consume the pipeline? Each correct answer presents part of the solution.

NOTE: Each correct selection is worth one point.

A. the model name

B. the training endpoint

C. the authentication key

D. the REST endpoint

Answer: AD

Question 52. For each of the following statements, select Yes if the statement is true. Otherwise, select No. NOTE: Each correct selection is worth one point.

Statements	Yes	No
A. Automated machine learning provides you with the ability to Include custom Python scripts in a training pipeline.		
B. Automated machine learning implements machine learning solutions without the need for programming experience.		
C. Automated machine learning provides you with the ability to visually connect datasets and modules on an interactive canvas.		

A. Mastered

B. Not Mastered

Answer: A

Question 53. You are building an AI system.

Which task should you include to ensure that the service meets the Microsoft transparency principle for responsible AI?

A. Ensure that all visuals have an associated text that can be read by a screen reader.

B. Enable autoscaling to ensure that a service-scales based on demand.

C. Provide documentation to help developers debug code.

D. Ensure that a training dataset is representative of the population.

Answer: C

Question 54. A company employs a team of customer service agents to provide telephone and email support to customers. The company develops a webchat bot to provide automated answers to common customer queries.

Which business benefit should the company expect as a result of creating the webchat bot solution?

A. increased sales

B. a reduced workload for the customer service agents

C. improved product reliability

Answer: B

Question 55. For a machine learning progress, how should you split data for training and evaluation?

A. Use features for training and labels for evaluation.

B. Randomly split the data into rows for training and rows for evaluation.

C. Use labels for training and features for evaluation.

D. Randomly split the data into columns for training and columns for evaluation.

Answer: D

Question 56. What are three Microsoft guiding principles for responsible AI? Each correct answer presents a complete solution.

NOTE: Each correct selection is worth one point.

A. knowledgeability

B. decisiveness

C. inclusiveness

D. fairness

E. opinionatedness

F. reliability and safety

Answer: CDF

Question 57. You use Azure Machine Learning designer to publish an inference pipeline.

Which two parameters should you use to consume the pipeline? Each correct answer presents part of the solution.

NOTE: Each correct selection is worth one point.

A. the model name

B. the training endpoint

C. the authentication key

D. the REST endpoint

Answer: AD

Question 58. For each of the following statements, select Yes if the statement is true. Otherwise, select No. NOTE: Each correct selection is worth one point.

Statements	Yes	No
A. Automated machine learning provides you with the ability to Include custom Python scripts in a training pipeline.		
B. Automated machine learning implements machine learning solutions without the need for programming experience.		
C. Automated machine learning provides you with the ability to visually connect datasets and modules on an interactive canvas.		

A. Mastered

B. Not Mastered

Answer: A

Question 59. You are designing an AI system that empowers everyone, including people who have hearing, visual, and other impairments.

This is an example of which Microsoft guiding principle for responsible AI?

A. fairness

B. inclusiveness

C. reliability and safety

D. accountability

Answer: B

Question 60. A company employs a team of customer service agents to provide telephone and email support to customers. The company develops a webchat bot to provide automated answers to common customer queries.

Which business benefit should the company expect as a result of creating the webchat bot solution?

A. increased sales

B. a reduced workload for the customer service agents

C. improved product reliability

Answer: B

Question 61. For a machine learning progress, how should you split data for training and evaluation?

A. Use features for training and labels for evaluation.

B. Randomly split the data into rows for training and rows for evaluation.

C. Use labels for training and features for evaluation.

D. Randomly split the data into columns for training and columns for evaluation.

Answer: D

Question 62. Your company is exploring the use of voice recognition technologies in its smart home devices. The company wants to identify any barriers that might unintentionally leave out specific user groups.

This an example of which Microsoft guiding principle for responsible AI?

A. accountability

B. fairness

C. inclusiveness

D. privacy and security

Answer: C

Question 63. For each of the following statements, select Yes if the statement is true. Otherwise, select No. NOTE: Each correct selection is worth one point.

Statements	Yes	No
A. Azure Machine Leaming designer provides a drag-and-drop visual canvas to build, test, and deploy machine learning models.		
B. Azure Machine Leaming designer enables you to save your progress as a pipeline draft		
C. Azure Machine Learning designer enables you to include custom JavaScript functions-		

A. Mastered

B. Not Mastered

Answer: A

Question 64. Which two components can you drag onto a canvas in Azure Machine Learning designer? Each correct answer presents a complete solution.

NOTE: Each correct selection is worth one point.

A. dataset

B. compute

C. pipeline

D. module

Answer: AD

Question 65. You use Azure Machine Learning designer to publish an inference pipeline.

Which two parameters should you use to consume the pipeline? Each correct answer presents part of the solution.

NOTE: Each correct selection is worth one point.

A. The model name

B. The training endpoint

C. The authentication key

D. The REST endpoint

Answer: AD

Question 66. For each of the following statements, select Yes if the statement is true. Otherwise, select No. NOTE: Each correct selection is worth one point

A. Mastered

B. Not Mastered

Answer: A

Question 67. You are building an AI system.

Which task should you include to ensure that the service meets the Microsoft transparency principle for responsible AI?

A. Ensure that all visuals have an associated text that can be read by a screen reader.

B. Enable autoscaling to ensure that a service-scales based on demand.

C. Provide documentation to help developers debug code.

D. Ensure that a training dataset is representative of the population.

Answer: C

Question 68. A company employs a team of customer service agents to provide telephone and email support to customers. The company develops a webchat bot to provide automated answers to common customer queries.

Which business benefit should the company expect as a result of creating the webchat bot solution?

A. increased sales

B. a reduced workload for the customer service agents

C. improved product reliability

Answer: B

Question 69. What are three Microsoft guiding principles for responsible AI? Each correct answer presents a complete solution.

NOTE: Each correct selection is worth one point.

A. knowledgeability

B. decisiveness

C. inclusiveness

D. fairness

E. opinionatedness

F. reliability and safety

Answer: CDF

Question 70. Which two components can you drag onto a canvas in Azure Machine Learning designer? Each correct answer presents a complete solution.

NOTE: Each correct selection is worth one point.

A. dataset

B. compute

C. pipeline

D. module

Answer: AD

Question 71. You need to predict the income range of a given customer by using the following dataset.

Which two fields should you use as features? Each correct answer presents a complete solution.

NOTE: Each correct selection is worth one point.

First Name	Last Name	Age	Educational Level	Income Range
Orlando	Gee	45	University	25,000-50,000
Keith	Harris	36	High school	25,000-50,000
Donna	Carreras	52	University	50,000-75,000
Janet	Gates	21	University	75,000-100,000
Lucy	Harrington	68	High school	50,000-75,000

A. Education Level

B. Last Name

C. Age

D. Income Range

E. First Name

Answer: AC

Question 72. You are building an AI system.

Which task should you include to ensure that the service meets the Microsoft transparency principle for responsible AI?

A. Ensure that all visuals have an associated text that can be read by a screen reader.

B. Enable autoscaling to ensure that a service scales based on demand.

C. Provide documentation to help developers debug code.

D. Ensure that a training dataset is representative of the population.

Answer: C

Question 73. A company employs a team of customer service agents to provide telephone and email support to customers. The company develops a webchat bot to provide automated answers to common customer queries.

Which business benefit should the company expect as a result of creating the webchat bot solution?

A. increased sales

B. a reduced workload for the customer service agents

C. improved product reliability

Answer: B

Question 74. You build a machine learning model by using the automated machine learning user interface (UI). You need to ensure that the model meets the Microsoft transparency principle for responsible AI. What should you do?

A. Set Validation type to Auto.

B. Enable Explain best model.

C. Set Primary metric to accuracy.

D. Set Max concurrent iterations to 0.

Answer: B

Question 75. For each of the following statements, select Yes if the statement is true. Otherwise, select No.

NOTE: Each correct selection is worth one point.

A. Mastered

B. Not Mastered

Answer: A

Question 76. What are three Microsoft guiding principles for responsible AI? Each correct answer presents a complete solution.

NOTE: Each correct selection is worth one point.

A. knowledgeability

B. decisiveness

C. inclusiveness

D. fairness

E. opinionatedness

F. reliability and safety

Answer: CDF

Question 77. Which two components can you drag onto a canvas in Azure Machine Learning designer? Each correct answer presents a complete solution.

NOTE: Each correct selection is worth one point.

A. dataset

B. compute

C. pipeline

D. module

Answer: AD

Question 78. You use Azure Machine Learning designer to publish an inference pipeline.

Which two parameters should you use to access the web service? Each correct answer presents part of the solution.

NOTE: Each correct selection is worth one point.

A. the model name

B. the training endpoint

C. the authentication key

D. the REST endpoint

Question 79. For each of the following statements, select Yes if the statement is true. Otherwise, select No.

NOTE: Each correct selection is worth one point.

Hot Area:

Statements	Yes	No
A. Azure Machine Leaming designer provides a drag-and-drop visual canvas to build, test, and deploy machine learning models.		
B. Azure Machine Leaming designer enables you to save your progress as a pipeline draft		
C. Azure Machine Learning designer enables you to include custom JavaScript functions-		

Answer:

Statements	Yes / No
A. Azure Machine Leaming designer provides a drag-and-drop visual canvas to build, test, and deploy machine learning models.	Yes
B. Azure Machine Leaming designer enables you to save your progress as a pipeline draft	Yes
C. Azure Machine Learning designer enables you to include custom JavaScript functions-	No

Question 80. For each of the following statements, select Yes if the statement is true. Otherwise, select No.

NOTE: Each correct selection is worth one point.

Hot Area:

Statements	Yes	No
A. Automated machine learning provides you with the ability to Include custom Python scripts in a training pipeline.		
B. Automated machine learning implements machine learning solutions without the need for programming experience.		
C. Automated machine learning provides you with the ability to visually connect datasets and modules on an interactive canvas.		

Answer:

Statements	Yes/ No
A. Automated machine learning provides you with the ability to Include custom Python scripts in a training pipeline.	Yes
B. Automated machine learning implements machine learning solutions without the need for programming experience.	No
C. Automated machine learning provides you with the ability to visually connect datasets and modules on an interactive canvas.	No

Question 81. When training a model, why should you randomly split the rows into separate subsets?

A. to train the model twice to attain better accuracy

B. to train multiple models simultaneously to attain better performance

C. to test the model by using data that was not used to train the model

Answer: C

Question 82. You are evaluating whether to use a basic workspace or an enterprise workspace in Azure Machine Learning.

What are two tasks that require an enterprise workspace? Each correct answer presents a complete solution.

NOTE: Each correct selection is worth one point.

A. Use a graphical user interface (GUI) to run automated machine learning experiments.

B. Create a compute instance to use as a workstation.

C. Use a graphical user interface (GUI) to define and run machine learning experiments from Azure Machine Learning designer.

D. Create a dataset from a comma-separated value (CSV) file.

Answer: A, C

Question 83. You are building a tool that will process images from retail stores and identify the products of competitors.

The solution will use a custom model.

Which Azure Cognitive Services service should you use?

A. Custom Vision

B. Form Recognizer

C. Face

D. Computer Vision

Answer: A

Question 84. For each of the following statements, select Yes if the statement is true. Otherwise, select No.

NOTE: Each correct selection is worth one point.

Hot Area:

Statements	Yes	No
A. Organizing documents into groups based on similarities of the text contained in the documents is an example of clustering.		
B. Grouping similar patients based on symptoms and diagnostic test results is an example of clustering.		
C. Predicting whether a person will develop mild, moderate, or severe allergy symptoms based on pollen count is an example of clustering.		

Answer:

Statements	Yes/ NO
A. Organizing documents into groups based on similarities of the text contained in the documents is an example of clustering.	Yes
B. Grouping similar patients based on symptoms and diagnostic test results is an example of clustering.	Yes
C. Predicting whether a person will develop mild, moderate, or severe allergy symptoms based on pollen count is an example of clustering.	NO

Question 85. For each of the following statements, select Yes if the statement is true. Otherwise, select No.

NOTE: Each correct selection is worth one point.

Hot Area:

Statements	Yes	No
A. A validation set includes the set of input examples that will be used to train a mode.		
B. A validation set can be used to determine how well a model predicts labels.		
C. A validation set can be used to verify that all the training data was used to train the model.		

Answer:

Statements	Yes/ No
A. A validation set includes the set of input examples that will be used to train a mode.	No
B. A validation set can be used to determine how well a model predicts labels.	Yes
C. A validation set can be used to verify that all the training data was used to train the model.	No

Question 86. What are two metrics that you can use to evaluate a regression model? Each correct answer presents a complete solution.

NOTE: Each correct selection is worth one point.

A. coefficient of determination (R2)

B. F1 score

C. root mean squared error (RMSE)

D. area under curve (AUC)

E. balanced accuracy

Answer: A, C

Question 87. Which type of machine learning should you use to identify groups of people who have similar purchasing habits?

A. classification

B. regression

C. clustering

Answer: C

Question 88. Which metric can you use to evaluate a classification model?

A. true positive rate

B. mean absolute error (MAE)

C. coefficient of determination (R2)

D. root mean squared error (RMSE)

Answer: A

Question 89. Which two components can you drag onto a canvas in Azure Machine Learning designer? Each correct answer presents a complete solution.

NOTE: Each correct selection is worth one point.

A. dataset

B. compute

C. pipeline

D. module

Answer: A, D

Question 90. You need to create a training dataset and validation dataset from an existing dataset. Which module in the Azure Machine Learning designer should you use?

A. Select Columns in Dataset

B. Add Rows

C. Split Data

D. Join Data

Answer: C

Question 91. For each of the following statements, select Yes if the statement is true. Otherwise, select No.

NOTE: Each correct selection is worth one point.

Hot Area:

Statements	Yes	No
A. You train a regression model by using unlabeled data.		
B. The classification technique is used to predict sequential numerical data over time.		
C. Grouping items by their common characteristics is an example of clustering.		

Answer:

Statements	Yes/ No
A. You train a regression model by using unlabeled data.	No
B. The classification technique is used to predict sequential numerical data over time.	No
C. Grouping items by their common characteristics is an example of clustering.	Yes

Question 92. Which two actions are performed during the data ingestion and data preparation stage of an Azure Machine Learning process? Each correct answer presents part of the solution.

NOTE: Each correct selection is worth one point.

A. Calculate the accuracy of the model.

B. Score test data by using the model.

C. Combine multiple datasets.

D. Use the model for real-time predictions.

E. Remove records that have missing values.

Question 93. You need to predict the animal population of an area.

Which Azure Machine Learning type should you use?

A. regression

B. clustering

C. classification

Answer: A

Question 94. Which two languages can you use to write custom code for Azure Machine Learning designer? Each correct answer presents a complete solution.

NOTE: Each correct selection is worth one point.

A. Python

B. R

C. C#

D. Scala

Answer: A, B

Question 95. Your company wants to build a recycling machine for bottles. The recycling machine must automatically identify bottles of the correct shape and reject all other items.

Which type of AI workload should the company use?

A. anomaly detection

B. conversational AI

C. computer vision

D. natural language processing

Answer: C

Question 96. For each of the following statements, select Yes if the statement is true. Otherwise, select No.

NOTE: Each correct selection is worth one point.

Hot Area:

Statements	Yes	No
A. When creating an object detection model in the Custom Vision service, you must choose a classification type of either Multilabel or Multiclass.		
B. You can create an object detection model in the Custom Vision service to find the location of content within an image.		
C. When creating an object detection model in the Custom Vision service, you can select from a set of predefined domains.		

Answer:

Statements	Yes/ No
A. When creating an object detection model in the Custom Vision service, you must choose a classification type of either Multilabel or Multiclass.	No
B. You can create an object detection model in the Custom Vision service to find the location of content within an image.	Yes
C. When creating an object detection model in the Custom Vision service, you can select from a set of predefined domains.	Yes

Question 97. In which two scenarios can you use the Form Recognizer service? Each correct answer presents a complete solution.

NOTE: Each correct selection is worth one point.

A. Extract the invoice number from an invoice.

B. Translate a form from French to English.

C. Find image of product in a catalog.

D. Identify the retailer from a receipt.

Answer: A, D

Question 98. You have a database that contains a list of employees and their photos.

You are tagging new photos of the employees.

For each of the following statements select Yes if the statement is true. Otherwise, select No.

NOTE: Each correct selection is worth one point.

Hot Area:

Statements	Yes	No
A. The Face service can be used to perform facial recognition for employees		
B. The Face service will be more accurate if you provide more sample photos of each employee from different angles.		
C. If an employee is wearing sunglasses, the Face service will always fail to recognize the employee.		

Answer:

Statements	Yes/ No
A. The Face service can be used to perform facial recognition for employees	Yes
B. The Face service will be more accurate if you provide more sample photos of each employee from different angles.	Yes
C. If an employee is wearing sunglasses, the Face service will always fail to recognize the employee.	No

Question 99. You need to develop a mobile app for employees to scan and store their expenses while travelling.

Which type of computer vision should you use?

A. semantic segmentation

B. image classification

C. object detection

D. optical character recognition (OCR)

Answer: D

Question 100. For each of the following statements, select Yes if the statement is true. Otherwise, select No.

NOTE: Each correct selection is worth one point.

Hot Area:

Statements	Yes	No
A. The Custom Vision service can be used to detect objects in an image.		
B. The Custom Vision service requires that you provide your own data to train the model.		
C. The Custom Vision service can be used to analyze video files.		

Answer:

Statements	Yes/ No
A. The Custom Vision service can be used to detect objects in an image.	Yes
B. The Custom Vision service requires that you provide your own data to train the model.	Yes
C. The Custom Vision service can be used to analyze video files.	No

Question 101. You are processing photos of runners in a race.

You need to read the numbers on the runners' shirts to identity the runners in the photos.

Which type of computer vision should you use?

A. facial recognition

B. optical character recognition (OCR)

C. image classification

D. object detection

Answer: B

Question 102. You need to determine the location of cars in an image so that you can estimate the distance between the cars.

Which type of computer vision should you use?

A. optical character recognition (OCR)

B. object detection

C. image classification

D. face detection

Answer: B

Question 103. What are two tasks that can be performed by using the Computer Vision service? Each correct answer presents a complete solution.

NOTE: Each correct selection is worth one point.

A. Train a custom image classification model.

B. Detect faces in an image.

C. Recognize handwritten text.

D. Translate the text in an image between languages.

Answer: B, C

Question 104. You need to build an image tagging solution for social media that tags images of your friends automatically.

Which Azure Cognitive Services service should you use?

A. Face

B. Form Recognizer

C. Text Analytics

D. Computer Vision

Answer: A

Question 105. In which two scenarios can you use the Form Recognizer service? Each correct answer presents a complete solution.

NOTE: Each correct selection is worth one point.

A. Identify the retailer from a receipt

B. Translate from French to English

C. Extract the invoice number from an invoice

D. Find images of products in a catalog

Answer: A, C

Question 106. Which Computer Vision feature can you use to generate automatic captions for digital photographs?

A. Recognize text.

B. Identify the areas of interest.

C. Detect objects.

D. Describe the images.

Answer: D

Question 107. Which service should you use to extract text, key/value pairs, and table data automatically from scanned documents?

A. Custom Vision

B. Face

C. Form Recognizer

D. Language

Answer: C

Question 108. You are developing a solution that uses the Text Analytics service.

You need to identify the main talking points in a collection of documents.

Which type of natural language processing should you use?

A. entity recognition

B. key phrase extraction

C. sentiment analysis

D. language detection

Answer: B

Question 109. In which two scenarios can you use speech recognition? Each correct answer presents a complete solution.

NOTE: Each correct selection is worth one point.

A. an in-car system that reads text messages aloud

B. providing closed captions for recorded or live videos

C. creating an automated public address system for a train station

D. creating a transcript of a telephone call or meeting

Answer: B, D

Question 110. You need to build an app that will read recipe instructions aloud to support users who have reduced vision.

Which version service should you use?

A. Text Analytics

B. Translator

C. Speech

D. Language Understanding (LUIS)

Answer: C

Question 111. For each of the following statements, select Yes if the statement is true. Otherwise, select No.

NOTE: Each correct selection is worth one point.

Hot Area:

Statements	Yes	No
A. You can use the Speech service to transcribe a call to text.		
B. You can use the Text Analytics service to extract key entities from a call transcript		
C. You can use the Speech service to translate the audio of a call to a different language.		

Answer:

Statements	Yes/ No
A. You can use the Speech service to transcribe a call to text.	Yes
B. You can use the Text Analytics service to extract key entities from a call transcript	Yes
C. You can use the Speech service to translate the audio of a call to a different language.	Yes

Question 112. Your website has a chatbot to assist customers.

You need to detect when a customer is upset based on what the customer types in the chatbot.

Which type of AI workload should you use?

A. anomaly detection

B. computer vision

C. regression

D. natural language processing

Answer: D

Question 113. You plan to develop a bot that will enable users to query a knowledge base by using natural language processing.

Which two services should you include in the solution? Each correct answer presents part of the solution.

NOTE: Each correct selection is worth one point.

A. QnA Maker

B. Azure Bot Service

C. Form Recognizer

D. Anomaly Detector

Answer: A, B

Question 114. In which two scenarios can you use a speech synthesis solution? Each correct answer presents a complete solution.

NOTE: Each correct selection is worth one point.

A. an automated voice that reads back a credit card number entered into a telephone by using a numeric keypad

B. generating live captions for a news broadcast

C. extracting key phrases from the audio recording of a meeting

D. an AI character in a computer game that speaks audibly to a player

Answer: A, D

Question 115. For each of the following statements, select Yes if the statement is true. Otherwise, select No.

NOTE: Each correct selection is worth one point.

Hot Area:

Statements	Yes	No
A. You can use the Translator service to translate text between languages.		
B. You can use the Translator service to detect the language of a given text.		
C. You can use the Translator service to transcribe audible speech into text.		

Answer:

Statements	Yes/ No
A. You can use the Translator service to translate text between languages.	Yes
B. You can use the Translator service to detect the language of a given text.	Yes
C. You can use the Translator service to transcribe audible speech into text.	No

Question 116. You are building a knowledge base by using QnA Maker.

Which file format can you use to populate the knowledge base?

A. PPTX

B. XML

C. ZIP

D. PDF

Answer: D

Question 117. In which scenario should you use key phrase extraction?

A. identifying whether reviews of a restaurant are positive or negative

B. generating captions for a video based on the audio track

C. identifying which documents provide information about the same topics

D. translating a set of documents from English to German

Answer: C

Question 118. You have insurance claim reports that are stored as text.

You need to extract key terms from the reports to generate summaries.

Which type of AI workload should you use?

A. natural language processing

B. conversational AI

C. anomaly detection

D. computer vision

Answer: A

Question 119. You are developing a chatbot solution in Azure.

Which service should you use to determine a user's intent?

A. Translator

B. QnA Maker

C. Speech

D. Language Understanding (LUIS)

Answer: D

Question 120. For each of the following statements, select Yes if the statement is true. Otherwise, select No.

NOTE: Each correct selection is worth one point.

Hot Area:

Statements	Yes	No
A. The Text Analytics service can identify in which language text is written.		
B. The Text Analytics service can detect handwritten signatures in a document.		
C. The Text Analytics service can identify companies and organizations mentioned in a document.		

Answer:

Statements	Yes/ No
A. The Text Analytics service can identify in which language text is written.	Yes
B. The Text Analytics service can detect handwritten signatures in a document.	No
C. The Text Analytics service can identify companies and organizations mentioned in a document.	Yes

Question 121. You are developing a natural language processing solution in Azure. The solution will analyze customer reviews and determine how positive or negative each review is.

This is an example of which type of natural language processing workload?

A. language detection

B. sentiment analysis

C. key phrase extraction

D. entity recognition

Answer: B

Question 122. You are authoring a Language Understanding (LUIS) application to support a music festival.

You want users to be able to ask questions about scheduled shows, such as: `Which act is playing on the main stage?`

The question `Which act is playing on the main stage?` is an example of which type of element?

A. an intent

B. an utterance

C. a domain

D. an entity

Answer: B

Question 123. You build a QnA Maker bot by using a frequently asked questions (FAQ) page.

You need to add professional greetings and other responses to make the bot more user friendly.

What should you do?

A. Increase the confidence threshold of responses

B. Enable active learning

C. Create multi-turn questions

D. Add chit-chat

Answer: D

Question 124. You need to develop a chatbot for a website. The chatbot must answer users' questions based on the information in the following documents:

➯ A product troubleshooting guide in a Microsoft Word document

➯ A frequently asked questions (FAQ) list on a webpage

Which service should you use to process the documents?

A. Azure Bot Service

B. Language Understanding

C. Text Analytics

D. QnA Maker

Answer: D

Question 125. You are building a Language Understanding model for an e-commerce business. You need to ensure that the model detects when utterances are outside the intended scope of the model.

What should you do?

A. Test the model by using new utterances

B. Add utterances to the None intent

C. Create a prebuilt task entity

D. Create a new model

Answer: B

Question 126. Which type of artificial intelligence workload uses sensors to proactively alert users about

potential equipment mechanical failures?

A. Anomaly detection

B. Computer vision

C. Natural language processing

D. Conversational AI

Answer: A

Question 127. The principle that describes raising awareness of the limitations of responsible AI-based
solutions is called: ________________.

A. Privacy and security

B. Reliability and safety

C. Transparency

D. Accountability

Answer: C

Question 128. The principle of providing the benefits of responsible AI systems to all parts of society regardless
of their gender or ethnicity is called: ____________.

A. Privacy and security

B. Reliability and safety

C. Inclusiveness

D. Accountability

Answer: C

Question 129. You need to identify numerical values that represent the probability of dogs becoming ill based
on their age and body fat percentage.

Which type of machine learning model should you use?

A. Linear regression

B. Multiple linear regression

C. Logistic regression

D. Hierarchical clustering

Answer: B

Question 130. You plan to use machine learning to predict how ill dogs become based on their age and body
fat percentage.

The model should include ___________.

A. two features and one label

B. two labels and one feature

C. three labels

D. three features

Answer: A

Question 131. You create a multiclass classification model.

You need to evaluate the model.

Which two evaluation metrics can you use? Each correct answer presents a complete solution.

A. F1 score

B. Accuracy

C. Rand index

D. Mean Squared Error (MSE)

Answer: A, B

Question 132. You train an Azure Machine Learning model and plan to deploy the model as a predictive
service in a production environment.

You must create an inference cluster before you deploy the model to _______________.

A. Azure Kubernetes Service

B. Azure Container Instance

C. Azure Function

D. Azure Logic Apps

Answer: A

Question 133. You plan to build and deploy a predictive model by using AutoML UI in Azure Machine Learning.

Which three machine learning tasks are supported? Each correct answer presents a complete solution.

A. Classification

B. Regression

C. Forecasting

D. Clustering

E. Reinforcement learning

Answer: A, B. C

Question 134. Which technique serves as the basis for modern image classification solutions?

A. Deep learning

B. Anomaly detection

C. Linear regression

D. Multiple linear regression

Answer: A

Question 135. You can extract information printed on food product labels by using ______________________.

A. image classification

B. natural language processing

C. optical character recognition

D. image segmentation

Answer: C

Question 136. What are two capabilities of the Azure Computer Vision service? Each correct answer presents a

complete solution.

A. Class prediction

B. Model training

C. Model authoring

D. Data visualization

E. Data exploration

Answer: A, B

Question 137. You need to train a machine learning model to detect company logos in images.

What should you use?

A. Azure Custom Vision image classification

B. Azure Custom Vision object detection

C. Azure Face Service

D. Language Understanding Intelligent Service (LUIS)

Answer: B

Question 138. You need to collect the names of people, organizations, and events from a set of PDF

documents.

Which natural language processing feature should you use?

A. Extractive summarization

B. Sentiment analysis

C. Named entity recognition

D. Key phrase extraction

Answer: C

Question 139. Which three capabilities does Azure Cognitive Services Text Analytics service support? Each

correct answer presents a complete solution.

A. Unlimited document size

B. All world languages

C. Chatbot integration

D. Multilingual content

E. Confidence scoring

Answer: C, D, E

Question 140. You need to identify users based on their voice.

Which Azure Speech service feature should you use?

A. Conversation transcription

B. Pronunciation assessment

C. Language Understanding Intelligent Service (LUIS)

D. Speaker recognition

Answer: D

Question 150. Select the answer that correctly completes the sentence.

You can exchange chatbot activities with other services by implementing ________________.

A. cards

B. channels

C. dialog

D. turns

Answer: B

Question 151. You develop a chatbot by using a Cognitive Services custom question answering project.

You need to add a personality to the chatbot.

What should you do?

A. Provide a default answer.

B. Add chitchat to the knowledge base.

C. Increase the Cognitive Search resource pricing tier limit.

D. Add hero cards to the chatbot.

Answer: B

Question 152. A company employs a team of customer service agents to provide telephone and email support to

customers.

The company develops a webchat bot to provide automated answers to common customer queries.

Which business benefit should the company expect as a result of creating the webchat bot solution?

A. increased sales

B. a reduced workload for the customer service agents

C. improved product reliability

Answer: B

Question 153. For a machine learning progress, how should you split data for training and evaluation?

A. Use features for training and labels for evaluation.

B. Randomly split the data into rows for training and rows for evaluation.

C. Use labels for training and features for evaluation.

D. Randomly split the data into columns for training and columns for evaluation

Answer: B

Question 154. You build a machine learning model by using the automated machine learning user interface (UI).

You need to ensure that the model meets the Microsoft transparency principle for responsible AI.

What should you do?

A. Set Validation type to Auto.

B. Enable Explain best model.

C. Set Primary metric to accuracy.

D. Set Max concurrent iterations to 0

Answer: B

Question 155. You have an Internet of Things (loT) device that monitors engine temperature.

The device generates an alert if the engine temperature deviates from expected norms.

Which type of Al workload does the device represent?

A. Natural language processing (NLP)

B. Computer vision

C. Anomaly detection

D. Knowledge mining

Answer: C

Question 156. You have a website that includes customer reviews.

You need to store the reviews in English and present the reviews to users in their respective language by recognizing each users geographical location.

Which type of natural language processing workload should you use?

A. Translation

B. Language modeling

C. Key phrase extraction

D. Speech recognition

Answer: C

Question 160. For which two workloads can you use computer vision? Each correct answer presents a complete solution. NOTE: Each correct selection is worth one point.

A. Creating photorealistic images by using three-dimensional models

B. Assigning the color pixels in an image to object names

C. Describing the contents of an image

D. Detecting inconsistencies and anomalies in a stream of data

E. Creating visual representations of numerical data

Answer: B, C

Question 161. Your company manufactures widgets.

You have 1.000 digital photos of the widgets.

You need to identify the location of the widgets within the photos.

What should you use?

A. Computer Vision Spatial Analysis

B. Custom Vision object detection

C. Custom Vision classification

D. Computer Vision Image Analysis

Answer: B

Question 162. You have a custom question answering solution.

You create a bot that uses the knowledge base to respond to customer requests. You need to identify what the bot can perform without adding additional skills. What should you identify?

A. Register customer complaints.

B. Answer questions from multiple users simultaneously.

C. Register customer purchases.

D. Provide customers with return materials authorization (RMA) numbers.

Answer: B

Question 163. A company employs a team of customer service agents to provide telephone and email support to

customers.

The company develops a webchat bot to provide automated answers to common customer queries. Which business benefit should the company expect as a result of creating the webchat bot solution?

A. increased sales

B. a reduced workload for the customer service agents

C. improved product reliability

Answer: B

Question 164. For a machine learning progress, how should you split data for training and evaluation?

A. Use features for training and labels for evaluation.

B. Randomly split the data into rows for training and rows for evaluation.

C. Use labels for training and features for evaluation.

D. Randomly split the data into columns for training and columns for evaluation

Answer: B

Question 165. Your company is exploring the use of voice recognition technologies in its smart home devices. The company wants to identify any barriers that might unintentionally leave out specific user groups.

This an example of which Microsoft guiding principle for responsible AI?

A. Accountability

B. Fairness

C. Inclusiveness

D. Privacy and security

Answer: C

Question 166. What are three Microsoft guiding principles for responsible AI? Each correct answer presents a complete solution.

NOTE: Each correct selection is worth one point.

A. Knowledgeability

B. Decisiveness

C. Inclusiveness

D. Fairness

E. Opinionatedness

F. Reliability and safety

Answer: C, D, F

Question 167. Which two components can you drag onto a canvas in Azure Machine Learning designer? Each correct answer presents a complete solution.

NOTE: Each correct selection is worth one point.

A. dataset

B. compute

C. pipeline

D. module

Answer: A, D

Question 168. For a machine learning progress, how should you split data for training and evaluation?

Use features for training and labels for evaluation.

Randomly split the data into rows for training and rows for evaluation.

Use labels for training and features for evaluation.

Randomly split the data into columns for training and columns for evaluation.

Answer: B

Question 169. You build a machine learning model by using the automated machine learning user interface (UI).

You need to ensure that the model meets the Microsoft transparency principle for responsible AI.

What should you do?

Set Validation type to Auto.

Enable Explain best model.

Set Primary metric to accuracy.

Set Max concurrent iterations to 0.

Answer: B

Question 170. You are building an AI system.

Which task should you include to ensure that the service meets the Microsoft transparency principle for responsible AI?

Ensure that all visuals have an associated text that can be read by a screen reader.

Enable autoscaling to ensure that a service scales based on demand.

Provide documentation to help developers debug code.

Ensure that a training dataset is representative of the population.

Question 171. What are three Microsoft guiding principles for responsible AI? Each correct answer presents a complete solution.

Note: Each correct selection is worth one point.

knowledgeability

decisiveness

inclusiveness

fairness

opinionatedness

reliability and safety

Answer: C, D, F

Question 172. You run a charity event that involves posting photos of people wearing sunglasses on Twitter.

You need to ensure that you only retweet photos that meet the following requirements:

Include one or more faces.

Contain at least one person wearing sunglasses.

What should you use to analyze the images?

A. the Verify operation in the Face service

B. the Detect operation in the Face service

C. the Describe Image operation in the Computer Vision service

D. the Analyze Image operation in the Computer Vision service

Answer: B

Question 173. You are building an AI-based app.

You need to ensure that the app uses the principles for responsible AI.

Which two principles should you follow? Each correct answer presents part of the solution.

Note: Each correct selection is worth one point.

A. Implement an Agile software development methodology

B. Implement a process of AI model validation as part of the software review process

C. Establish a risk governance committee that includes members of the legal team, members of the risk management team, and a privacy officer

D. Prevent the disclosure of the use of AI-based algorithms for automated decision making

Answer: B, C

Question 174. A company employs a team of customer service agents to provide telephone and email support to customers.

The company develops a webchat bot to provide automated answers to common customer queries. Which business benefit should the company expect as a result of creating the webchat bot solution?

A: increased sales

B: a reduced workload for the customer service agents

C: improved product reliability

Answer: B

Question 175. For a machine learning progress, how should you split data for training and evaluation?

A: Use features for training and labels for evaluation.

B: Randomly split the data into rows for training and rows for evaluation.

C: Use labels for training and features for evaluation.

D: Randomly split the data into columns for training and columns for evaluation.

Answer: B

Question 176. You build a machine learning model by using the automated machine learning user interface (UI).

You need to ensure that the model meets the Microsoft transparency principle for responsible AI.

What should you do?

A: Set Validation type to Auto.

B: Enable Explain best model.

C: Set Primary metric to accuracy.

D: Set Max concurrent iterations to 0.

Answer: B

Question 177. You are designing an AI system that empowers everyone, including people who have hearing, visual, and other impairments.

This is an example of which Microsoft guiding principle for responsible AI?

A: fairness

B: inclusiveness

C: reliability and safety

D: accountability

Answer: B

Question 178. You are building an AI system.

Which task should you include to ensure that the service meets the Microsoft transparency principle for responsible AI?

A: Ensure that all visuals have an associated text that can be read by a screen reader.

B: Enable autoscaling to ensure that a service scales based on demand.

C: Provide documentation to help developers debug code.

D: Ensure that a training dataset is representative of the population.

Answer: C

Question 179. You run a charity event that involves posting photos of people wearing sunglasses on Twitter.

You need to ensure that you only retweet photos that meet the following requirements:

Include one or more faces.

Contain at least one person wearing sunglasses.

What should you use to analyze the images?

A: the Verify operation in the Face service

B: the Detect operation in the Face service

C: the Describe Image operation in the Computer Vision service

D: the Analyze Image operation in the Computer Vision service

Answer: B

Question180. For a machine learning progress, how should you split data for training and evaluation?

A: Use features for training and labels for evaluation.

B: Randomly split the data into rows for training and rows for evaluation.

C: Use labels for training and features for evaluation.

D: Randomly split the data into columns for training and columns for evaluation.

Answer: B

Question 181. You build a machine learning model by using the automated machine learning user interface (UI).

You need to ensure that the model meets the Microsoft transparency principle for responsible AI.

What should you do?

A: Set Validation type to Auto.

B: Enable Explain best model.

C: Set Primary metric to accuracy.

D: Set Max concurrent iterations to 0.

Answer: B

Question 182. You run a charity event that involves posting photos of people wearing sunglasses on Twitter.

You need to ensure that you only retweet photos that meet the following requirements:

Include one or more faces.

Contain at least one person wearing sunglasses.

What should you use to analyze the images?

A: the Verify operation in the Face service

B: the Detect operation in the Face service

C: the Describe Image operation in the Computer Vision service

D: the Analyze Image operation in the Computer Vision service

Correct **Answer:** B

Question 183. For a machine learning progress, how should you split data for training and evaluation?

A: Use features for training and labels for evaluation.

B: Randomly split the data into rows for training and rows for evaluation.

C: Use labels for training and features for evaluation.

D: Randomly split the data into columns for training and columns for evaluation.

Answer: D

Question 184. You build a machine learning model by using the automated machine learning user interface (UI).

You need to ensure that the model meets the Microsoft transparency principle for responsible AI.

What should you do?

A: Set Validation type to Auto.

B: Enable Explain best model.

C: Set Primary metric to accuracy.

D: Set Max concurrent iterations to 0.

Answer: B

Question 185. Which service should you use to extract text, key/value pairs, and table data automatically from scanned documents?

A: Form Recognizer

B: Text Analytics

C: Ink Recognizer

D: Custom Vision

Answer: A

Question 186. You use Azure Machine Learning designer to publish an inference pipeline.

Which two parameters should you use to consume the pipeline? Each correct answer presents part of the solution.

NOTE: Each correct selection is worth one point.

A: the model name

B: the training endpoint

C: the authentication key

D: the REST endpoint

Answer: A, D

Question 187. Which metric can you use to evaluate a classification model?

A: true positive rate

B: mean absolute error (MAE)

C: coefficient of determination (R2)

D: root mean squared error (RMSE)

Answer: A

Question 188. Which two components can you drag onto a canvas in Azure Machine Learning designer? Each correct answer presents a complete solution.

NOTE: Each correct selection is worth one point.

A: dataset

B: compute

C: pipeline

D: module

Answer: A, D

Question 189. You need to create a training dataset and validation dataset from an existing dataset. Which module in the Azure Machine Learning designer should you use?

A: Select Columns in Dataset

B: Add Rows

C: Split Data

D: Join Data

Answer: C

Question 190. For a machine learning progress, how should you split data for training and evaluation?

A: Use features for training and labels for evaluation.

B: Randomly split the data into rows for training and rows for evaluation.

C: Use labels for training and features for evaluation.

D: Randomly split the data into columns for training and columns for evaluation.

Answer: B

ONLINE RESOURCES

Practice Paper

Link : https://forms.office.com/r/k4wCjYFi1p

QR Code :

Video Content

Link : https://youtu.be/pDVjm8d-8ps

QR Code :

Chapter 5: Viva Voce Questions

Question 1: What is the primary purpose of Azure AI Fundamentals AI-900 certification?

Answer: The AI-900 certification aims to validate foundational knowledge related to artificial intelligence and machine learning on Azure, covering basic concepts, AI workloads, and considerations on Azure services.

Question 2: Can you explain what Machine Learning (ML) on Azure encompasses?

Answer: Machine Learning on Azure includes services and tools for building, training, and deploying ML models efficiently using Azure Machine Learning service, a cloud-based platform.

Question 3: What are Azure Cognitive Services?

Answer: Azure Cognitive Services are a suite of APIs, SDKs, and services available to developers to make their applications more intelligent, engaging, and discoverable by embedding the ability to see, hear, speak, understand, and interpret needs using natural methods of communication.

Question 4: Describe the role of Computer Vision in Azure AI.

Answer: Computer Vision in Azure AI provides tools to analyze content within images and videos to automatically generate descriptions, identify objects and faces, and perform advanced image processing.

Question 5: What is Azure Bot Service and its significance?

Answer: Azure Bot Service enables the creation and management of intelligent bots to interact with users in a natural way, using text, graphics, or speech. It is significant for automating customer services, enhancing user interaction, and scaling operations.

Question 6: How does Natural Language Processing (NLP) function within Azure AI?

Answer: NLP on Azure AI utilizes Language Understanding (LUIS) and Text Analytics to process and analyze text for tasks such as sentiment analysis, key phrase extraction, and language detection, enabling applications to understand human language.

Question 7: Discuss Azure's approach to ensuring ethics and privacy in AI deployments.

Answer: Azure commits to ethical AI by providing guidelines and governance frameworks, ensuring AI systems are fair, reliable, safe, private, and inclusive. It includes tools for monitoring and controlling AI deployments to adhere to privacy laws and regulations.

Question 8: What is the Azure ML Studio and its key features?

Answer: Azure ML Studio is an interactive, visual workspace designed to build, test, and deploy machine learning solutions without needing extensive programming, offering drag-and-drop model building and easy deployment options.

Question 9: Can you explain the concept of knowledge mining in Azure AI?

Answer: Knowledge mining is the process of using AI to ingest, enrich, and explore diverse content to discover latent insights. Azure provides tools like Azure Search and Form Recognizer for implementing knowledge mining workflows.

Question 10: What types of AI workloads are typically handled by Azure AI?

Answer: Azure AI handles workloads such as anomaly detection, computer vision, natural language processing, and predictive analytics, supporting a wide range of applications from business analytics to consumer services.

Question 11: How does Azure AI integrate with other Azure services?

Answer: Azure AI integrates seamlessly with other Azure services such as Azure Data Services for data storage and processing, Azure IoT for edge computing, and Azure Kubernetes Service for scaling applications.

Question 12: Describe a scenario where Azure AI can be used in real-world applications.

Answer: Azure AI can be utilized in retail for personalized shopping experiences by analyzing customer data and preferences to provide product recommendations and targeted marketing.

Question 13: What are the considerations for choosing the right AI service on Azure for a project?

Answer: Considerations include the specific AI needs of the project, data privacy requirements, scalability needs, technical expertise of the team, and cost implications of the Azure services.

Question 14: How does Azure ensure the scalability of AI solutions?

Answer: Azure provides scalable cloud infrastructure that can dynamically adjust resources based on the demand of AI applications, ensuring efficient handling of workloads as they grow.

Question 15: What is the importance of data privacy and security in Azure AI?

Answer: Data privacy and security are critical in Azure AI to protect sensitive information, comply with regulations, and build trust with users by ensuring that data is securely stored and processed.

Question 16: Can Azure AI be used for predictive analytics?

Answer: Yes, Azure AI can perform predictive analytics using Azure Machine Learning and Data Bricks to analyze historical data, identify patterns, and make predictions about future trends.

Question 17: What is the potential impact of AI on business according to Azure AI?

Answer: AI has the potential to significantly impact businesses by enhancing efficiency, automating routine tasks, providing deeper insights from data, and creating new opportunities for innovation and customer engagement.

Question 18: How does Azure facilitate the development and deployment of AI applications?

Answer: Azure facilitates AI development through comprehensive development tools, pre-built AI services, and robust deployment options such as container services and managed platforms.

Question 19: What is the role of developers and data scientists in shaping Azure AI solutions?

Answer: Developers and data scientists play a critical role in designing, building, and refining Azure AI solutions, utilizing their expertise to tailor AI models and applications that meet specific business needs.

Question 20: How do continuous updates in Azure AI services affect existing deployments?

Answer: Continuous updates in Azure AI services can enhance features and improve performance but may require existing deployments to adapt or update to maintain compatibility and take full advantage of new capabilities.

YouTube Link for Viva Voce Questions:

https://www.youtube.com/playlist?list=PLzlh_31VWEFqDML5o-JuQCu5Y_cNTrMTv

QR Code:

YouTube Videos Playlists for all Microsoft Certifications Videos

Microsoft Azure AI Fundamentals AZ-900

Link: https://www.youtube.com/playlist?list=PLzlh_31VWEFq9KU8Gr0ISbfj-TW6k17f8

QR Code:

Microsoft Azure Administrator AZ-104 Microsoft Azure Virtual Desktop AZ-140

Link: https://www.youtube.com/playlist?list=PLzlh_31VWEFq7JHJMuPJZcw-XShaPrUYP

QR Code:

Microsoft Azure Virtual Desktop AZ-140

Link: https://www.youtube.com/playlist?list=PLzlh_31VWEFowmPK_ro41wiljGoGKexGI

QR Code:

Microsoft Azure Developer AZ-204

Link:

https://www.youtube.com/playlist?list=PLzlh_31VWEFqT72UPVCUi6rqRqLBuwMSr

QR Code:

Designing Microsoft Azure Infrastructure Solution AZ-305

Link:

https://www.youtube.com/playlist?list=PLzlh_31VWEFpTerOknh9kgL4eTbhQwDND

QR Code:

Microsoft Azure Devops Engineer AZ-400

Link: https://www.youtube.com/playlist?list=PLzlh_31VWEFpyUIe_DuaeIkcThEfMT_BT

QR Code:

Microsoft Azure Security Engineer AZ-500

Link:

https://www.youtube.com/playlist?list=PLzlh_31VWEFqFBJgQTPNucIO0wVJdjNmS

QR Code:

Microsoft Azure Network Engineer AZ-700

Link:

https://www.youtube.com/playlist?list=PLzlh_31VWEFowujgDl16YDCvsQtmKgEqL

QR Code:

Microsoft Azure Fundamentals AZ-900

Link: https://www.youtube.com/playlist?list=PLzlh_31VWEFpeXZ2p32R1zDsgcbV8kI1K

QR Code:

Microsoft Azure Data Engineer DP-203

Link: https://www.youtube.com/playlist?list=PLzlh_31VWEFp3XTNqoS60UAOzl8NVG-5z

QR Code:

Microsoft Azure Database Administrator DP- 300

Link: https://www.youtube.com/playlist?list=PLzlh_31VWEFpv-rmc2mbpoIqUOqVW_cIo

QR Code: